UBU REPERTORY THEATER PUBLICATIONS

Individual plays:

Swimming Pools at War by Yves Navarre, 1982.
Night Just Before the Forest and *Struggle of the Dogs and the Black*, by Bernard–Marie Koltès, 1982.
The Fetishist by Michel Tournier, 1983.
The Office by Jean–Paul Aron, 1983.
Far From Hagondange and *Vater Land, the Country of our Fathers* by Jean–Paul Wenzel, 1984.
Deck Chairs by Madeleine Laik, 1984.
The Passport and *The Door* by Pierre Bourgeade, 1984.
The Showman by Andrée Chedid, 1984.
Madame Knipper's Journey to Eastern Prussia by Jean–Luc Lagarce, 1984.
Family Portrait by Denise Bonal, 1985; new edition, 1992.
Passengers by Daniel Besnehard, 1985.
Cabale by Enzo Cormann, 1985.
Enough is Enough by Protais Asseng, 1986.
Monsieur Thôgô–gnigni by Bernard Dadié, 1985.
The Glorious Destiny of Marshal Nnikon Nniku by Tchicaya U Tam'si, 1986.
Parentheses of Blood by Sony Labou Tansi, 1986.
Intelligence Powder by Kateb Yacine, 1986.
The Sea Between Us by Denise Chalem, 1986.
Country Landscapes by Jacques–Pierre Amette, 1986.
Nowhere and A Man with Women by Reine Bartève, 1987.
The White Bear by Daniel Besnehard, 1992.
The Best of Schools by Jean–Marie Besset, 1992.
Jock by Jean–Louis Bourdon, 1992.
A Tempest by Aimé Césaire, 1993 (new edition).
The Free Zone and The Workroom by Jean–Claude Grumberg, preface by Michael R. Marrus, 1993.
A Modest Proposal by Tilly, preface by Tom Bishop, 1994.

Ubu Repertory Theater:1982–1992, A bilingual illustrated history with personal statements by various playwrights and theater personalities, 1992.

*Distributed by Ubu Repertory Theater, 15 West 28th Street, New York, NY 10001. All other titles distributed by Theatre Communications Group, 355 Lexington Avenue, New York, NY 10017.

Anthologies:

Afrique I: New plays from the Congo, Ivory Coast, Senegal and Zaire, including *The Daughter of the Gods* by Abdou Anta Kâ, *Equatorium* by Maxime N'Debeka, *Lost Voices* by Diur N'Tumb, *The Second Ark* by Sony Labou Tansi, and *The Eye* by Bernard Zadi Zaourou. Preface by George C. Wolfe. 1987. (Out of print).

The Paris Stage: Recent Plays: *A Birthday Present for Stalin* by Jean Bouchaud, *The Rest Have Got It Wrong* by Jean–Michel Ribes, *The Sleepless City* by Jean Tardieu, *Trumpets of Death* by Tilly, and *The Neighbors* by Michel Vinaver. Preface by Catherine Temerson and Françoise Kourilsky. 1988.

Plays by Women: An International Anthology: *A Picture Perfect Sky* by Denise Bonal, *Jocasta* by Michèle Fabien, *The Girls from the Five and Ten* by Abla Farhoud, *You Have Come Back* by Fatima Gallaire–Bourega, and *Your Handsome Captain* by Simone Schwarz–Bart. Preface by Catherine Temerson and Françoise Kourilsky. 1988, 1991. (Out of print).

Gay Plays: An International Anthology: *The Function* by Jean–Marie Besset, *A Tower Near Paris* and *Grand Finale* by Copi, *Return of the Young Hippolytus* by Hervé Dupuis, *Ancient Boys* by Jean–Claude van Itallie, and *The Lives and Deaths of Miss Shakespeare* by Liliane Wouters. Preface by Catherine Temerson and Françoise Kourilsky. 1989, 1991.

Theater and Politics: An International Anthology: *Black Wedding Candles for Blessed Antigone* by Sylvain Bemba, *A Season in the Congo* by Aimé Césaire, *Burn River Burn* by Jean–Pol Fargeau, *Olympe and the Executioner* by Wendy Kesselman and *Mephisto*, adapted from Klaus Mann by Ariane Mnouchkine. Preface by Erika Munk. 1990.

Afrique II: New Plays from Madagascar, Mauritania and Togo including *The Legend of Wagadu as Seen by Sia Yatabere* by Moussa Diagana, *The Crossroads* by Josué Kossi Efoui, *The Herd* by Charlotte–Arrisoa Rafenomanjato, *The Prophet and the President* by Jean–Luc Raharimanana and *The Singing Tortoise* and *Yevi's Adventures in Monsterland* by Sénouvo Agbota Zinsou. Preface by Henry Louis Gates, Jr. 1991.

New French–Language Plays: *The Orphan Muses* by Michel Marc Bouchard (Quebec), *Fire's Daughters* by Ina Césaire (Martinique), *The Ship* by Michèle Césaire (Martinique), *Talk About Love!* by Paul Emond (Belgium), *That Old Black Magic* by Koffi Kwahulé (Ivory Coast). Preface by Rosette C. Lamont. 1993.

Plays by Women: An International Anthology. Book 2: *The Orphanage* by Reine Bartève (France), *Game of Patience* by Abla Farhoud (Quebec/Liban), *The Widow Dylemma* by Werewere Liking (Cameroon), *The Tropical Breeze Hotel* by Maryse Condé (Guadeloupe), *Beware the Heart* by Denise Bonal (France). Preface by Ntozake Shange. 1994

Tilly

A Modest Proposal

translated by
Richard Miller

preface by
Tom Bishop

UBU REPERTORY THEATER PUBLICATIONS
NEW YORK

Ubu Repertory Theater Publications
General Editors: Françoise Kourilsky, Catherine Temerson
Assistant Editor: Cristina Strempel

Distributed by Theatre Communications Group
355 Lexington Avenue,New York, N.Y. 10017

Printed in the United States of America, 1994
Library of Congress Catalog Card Number: 94-78232
ISBN 0-913745-43-X

Price: $8.95

The publication of this book was made possible in part by a grant from the Cultural Services of the French Embassy, New York.

CONTENTS

PREFACE

For the past twenty or so years, theater in France has been remarkably fertile, dominated by talented directors working mainly in national or state subsidized theaters, who have regaled the public with innovative productions of modern and ancient classics.

Yet, throughout this period, one regularly hears the mournful refrain that there is a dearth of dramatists writing in French. In fact, experience proves otherwise, as anyone familiar with the productions presented by Ubu Repertory Theater can testify. Many excellent playwrights are being performed and are well-known to audiences in Paris and in the regional theaters: men and women, young and less young, from metropolitan France or from French-speaking countries or areas.

Among the most brilliant of these is Tilly. Though not a prolific author, his five plays in fifteen years have made a powerful impact. His is a strikingly original voice. With irony and minute observation, with a keen sense of theatricality, he dissects French society and, by extension, Western society in general. The production of *Charcuterie fine* in 1980 (it was presented in English by Ubu as *Delicatessen*, in a 1985 staged reading) revealed a brilliant, new talent. The play introduces us to an inarticulate lower middle class family—a butcher, his wife, and their ne'er do well son—three very simple characters, at first glance ill-equipped to hold center stage. Yet, their modest existences become fully viable, even tragic, in this short play whose drama and eventual violence builds coherently thanks to Tilly's keen understanding of the human psyche and thanks to his unerring sense of theater devoid of flashy stage effects. Guy Dumur, the late, highly respected critic for the weekly *Nouvel Observateur*, acclaimed *Charcuterie fine* as "...a modern tragedy which owes everything to the compact silence in which these 'good people' are trapped and which one will not soon forget."

Tilly followed *Charcuterie fine* with *Spaghetti bolognese* in 1982 and then scored another major triumph in 1985 with *Les Trompettes de la mort* (presented as *Trumpets of Death* by Ubu in a sterling workshop production at the Guggenheim Museum the following year and published by Ubu in its *Paris Stage* anthology). *La Maison des Jeanne et de la culture*, in 1986, had a lesser impact, but with his most recent play, *Y'a bon bamboula,* in 1987, Tilly took his place among France's foremost dramatists. The milieu is once again the lower middle class, in its mediocrity, its hypocrisy, its latent violence, its bigotry. This time, though, the author deals with an even more dangerous subject: the racism that permeates a segment of contemporary French society. That *Y'a bon bamboula* will have memorable resonances in the United States is proof that, however different racial bigotry may appear from one country to another, racism is racism, the same pernicious, degrading syndrome. The family of Tilly's play will be immediately recognizable by Americans; they are no different from some people in the U.S. and their shameful strategies for the exclusion of others are all too familiar to us. Nicole Garcia, French actress and film-maker, writes of this theater that "...we believe in his universe as one believes in an absolute reality. We can't avoid it, we can't distance ourselves from it. We are caught by the lacerating force of his silences and of his words." Continuing an artistic commitment, Ubu again presents this outstanding work to the American public, in production and print, in a new US translation by Richard Miller, entitled *A Modest Proposal.*

The originality of Tilly's theater resides in the fact that he turns his back on a century-long tendency towards non-realistic theater in France and embraces fully the fourth-wall convention familiar to realistic theater of bygone days. We are meant to believe fully in what happens on stage, in the room we see, with the fourth wall—the one separating the stage from the audience mysteriously become transparent so that we can watch as privileged voyeurs what "real" people are "really" doing and saying. But this is no mere reversal to outmoded forms of nineteenth-century realism.

The precise observation, the accent on the quotidian, the humble, and the painful yields a wider perspective, a tragic view of daily humiliation compounded by humor (yes, there *is* a great deal of humor!) which makes us wince with the pain of recognition. Tilly does not explain, he demonstrates, and he does so without stylization, with no theatrical tricks, with a purity of dramaturgy that makes us forget we are in the theater. His writing is not limited to the dialogue; it includes every gesture, every item of scenery, every silence. In such an atmosphere, his actors are no longer characters, they simply *are.* And Tilly's world is, as Michel Hermon (who directed Tilly's first plays) noted, without pity. Without Brechtian ideology or didacticism, he challenges us to think, to judge, to react.

Tilly has long been involved in theater; before writing plays, he was an actor—and he continues to act on the stage, and more recently in films. He has also taken to directing his own works. Like Brazilian soccer players, Brittany-born Tilly prefers using only his last name. But he does have a first name, François. But just call him Tilly. You will long remember this playwright who invites us to an entirely new, stunning experience in the theater.

TOM BISHOP
August 1994

A CONVERSATION WITH TILLY

TOM BISHOP: Many labels have been suggested to describe your work such as theater of the everyday and hyper-realism. How do you react to such points of view?

TILLY: I pay no attention to that. I am satisfied to write and direct plays, and that's all. And when people talk to me about naturalism, hyper-realism and the like, it's not my problem. I never think in these terms; I've never thought in these terms.

TB: Nevertheless, when you write a play and you direct it, it involves the fourth-wall convention and the stage/audience relationship. Looking at your plays, one feels that you do in fact use the fourth-wall convention—in a different way, to be sure, without reverting to naturalism. Are you aware of this use of convention and do you reflect on the stage/audience relationship?

TILLY: Not when I write, but I do when I direct. When I direct my plays, these matters become very important. What I do is to ask my actors not to "perform." It's as if there were only one person looking at them. During rehearsals, I am alone with them, perhaps with an assistant, we are two at most. I ask them to work as if someone were looking at them through a half-opened door or through a window or through a keyhole. It is voyeurism.

TB: The spectator becomes a privileged voyeur, then?

TILLY: Yes, that's how I approach it.

TB: And you ask your actors not to concern themselves with this voyeur, don't you?

TILLY: Yes, not to concern themselves with anything, as if they were alone, as if the public did not exist.

TB: Yet at the same time, it's the public that carries them in what they do.

TILLY: Of course. I have just directed *Charcuterie fine* in Lausanne and will do it again in Paris this Fall at the Théâtre de la Colline. It is the first play I wrote and this was the first time I staged it. There have been several projects to revive it, but I wanted to keep the rights for myself because I really felt like directing it. It is as timely now as it was fifteen years ago.

TB: When you wrote *Charcuterie fine*, for instance, did you have in mind some form of realism or naturalism in the lineage of Antoine[1], some notion of fourth-wall convention? I would imagine not, but I wonder just the same.

TILLY: No. When I was writing, not at all. I really didn't have these references because I don't have a great theater culture. Often I am asked about people I haven't even heard of.

TB: So you weren't encumbered by all that?

TILLY: No, I was not, except perhaps unconsciously, because I had after all worked a good deal in the theater as an actor and I was never really satisfied with what I did. But I was never satisfied either by the work of others, by their way of speaking; somehow, I found all that really bizarre.

TB: But now that you are also a director, surely you are familiar with Antoine's work, even if you didn't know him at the outset?

TILLY: Yes, I am, because when I studied theater, I learned a lot about Antoine.

TB: Neither you nor I ever saw Antoine's work, yet we both know enough about what he did to realize that what you try to do is not unrelated to his attempts to renew the theater, even if the two are very different. But it seems to me that no one can see *Charcuterie fine* and think of Antoine with respect to the *subject* of

(1)André Antoine, the founder of the Théâtre Libre in Paris in the last years of the nineteenth century. At the Théâtre Libre, Antoine reacted against the prevailing, vapid forms of theater and revolutionized dramatic performance with a new, realistic esthetic.

the play. For me the difference is that you deal with less obviously "dramatic" situations, less spectacular ones. When you work with your actors, it's as if you were working under a microscope. And your work with them is a cooperative effort.

TILLY: At least I try. There are actors who find things and to whom I therefore give a lot of leeway; but there are others who don't work that way. I don't really give them instructions in this area. I am very insistent when it comes to moving on stage, to gestures, the economy of gestures, of glances, of movements. Everything has to be very, very precise. I ask precision of them. From that point on, they are closely locked into their work, so to speak; it's as if we were working more and more on a tightrope. At the start, I lead them across a river on a wide bridge; by the end, we finish the crossing on a tightrope. That's where we need to get to: from that point on, they keep their balance in order not to fall into an excess, even two excesses. They could fall into a "boulevard" or commercial excess or into another one that is not really more intellectual, but, let's say, more theatrical.

TB: I assume that when you say "theatrical," you mean the word in quotation marks; it is almost pejorative, isn't it? If it is "theatrical" it is already removed from what you are aiming at.

TILLY: Yes, that's exactly it.

TB: Still, it is theater.

TILLY: Yes, of course, but not "theatrical."

TB: You have been described as having a passion for being exhaustive.

TILLY: I don't know what that means.

TB: You are supposed to have a passion for being exhaustive, obsessive with respect to the use of sets, stage accessories.

TILLY: Yes, that's true. If plays are not staged as written, it can be a catastrophe. When it comes to the banality of the dialogue, everything beyond the dialogue must be kept closely in check.

TB: It is difficult to speak of banality.

TILLY: Last year, I saw *Charcuterie fine* performed in a provincial theater where the play lasted 20 or 25 minutes longer than what I just did. Silences are extremely important.

TB: 20 to 25 minutes longer! You must have suffered.

TILLY: Yes, I did.

TB: Let's talk about *A Modest Proposal (Y'a bon bamboula)*. You may remember that we talked about it several years ago, and that I suggested then that your play should work well in the United States because the problems and the mentality involved are analogous, even if they are not quite the same, even if the frame of reference is not the same. You don't favor "Americanizing" it, do you, making it more recognizable for Americans?

TILLY: No, I don't think so. France was a colonial power in Africa. One could transpose the play to Vietnam for a production in the United States, but it's not the same form of racism and I don't see the advantage of doing it. In the play, only the protagonists know why the black man winds up going back to Africa. They treated him very badly, but no one else really knows. That is certainly a danger.

TB: Do you consider it to be a political play?

TILLY: Political or social, I don't know.

TB: But not political in that it involves some precise French scene? Like the people around Le Pen?[2]

(2) Jean-Marie Le Pen, the leader of the ultra-right Front National Party.

TILLY: Somewhat. It's closer to somewhere between Chirac and de Villiers[3]. But the young woman could be a follower of Le Pen.

TB: When you wrote the play, all that did not yet exist, I believe. Was Le Pen already a political force?

TILLY: Yes, I think so. I recall a round-table discussion in Avignon[4]. Someone spoke of Le Pen, he was being talked about. I remember that I didn't want to speak his name because I thought that he was already being given too much attention.

TB: That's right. That was the time when people thought it best not to talk about him because it helped him too much. Since then, he has helped himself...Can you tell me what playwrights interest you? Influenced you? Whom do you like to read? Whose plays do you like to see?

TILLY: I never go to the theater. Or very very rarely. I haven't lived in Paris for the past year and a half, and don't intend to live there again.

TB: But even when you started, was there no one...?

TILLY: Yes, I did go to the theater a great deal then, but for a good number of years now, I haven't been going any more.

TB: I might imagine that you were not indifferent to Chekhov, for instance.

TILLY: You're right. In fact, he was the first dramatist I appreciated. When I was in school, I liked neither Molière nor Corneille. But I liked Racine —I like him still, in fact. I find his language superb, extraordinary. And later on, when my studies were over,

(3) Jacques Chirac, Mayor of Paris and former Prime Minister, head of the R.P.R., the neo-Gaullist ruling majority party and Philippe de Villiers, a politician currently gathering political momentum on the right wing of the French political scene.

(4) The Theater Festival, held every summer in the southern French city, Avignon.

I really discovered Chekhov, it was fantastic. And then Ibsen. Those were the two, Chekhov and Ibsen.

TB: Do you know the theater of Franz-Xavier Kroetz and Botho Strauss?[5]

TILLY: No. I saw one play by Kroetz—I don't remember which one—but I only found out later that it was by Kroetz. It was very good.

TB: I ask you that because Kroetz especially is close to your universe, to your concerns, to your esthetics.

TILLY: I have been asked about him before. That was the only play of his I saw.

TB: That must have been *Through the Leaves*, a play with some similarities to *Charcuterie fine*. There is also a woman who owns a butcher shop. In any case, you and Kroetz, and to some degree Strauss are at the center of an important current in contemporary European theater.

TILLY: I saw one play by Strauss. The text seemed interesting but I didn't like the production. I found the staging boring.

TB: Are you writing a play right now?

TILLY: No, I am doing a film, my second film. I haven't written a play for some time. I simply don't write for the theater anymore.

TB: You mean the theater is finished for you?

TILLY: I don't know. I have been on this film for a while; it takes a long time. And then, all I want now is to live in Brittany and write. Last year I began a play, and then I stopped. There are things I want to do, but what bothers me more and more is what

(5) Contemporary German playwrights.

comes afterwards, that is, try to get a production together, to stage the play. I don't really much feel like doing that any more, in Paris or elsewhere. What I do feel like doing now is to write.

TB: Well, I look forward to seeing you again this Fall, in New York, when you will come for the production of *A Modest Proposal* at Ubu.

Summer, 1994

A Modest Proposal, in Richard Miller's translation, had its American premiere at Ubu Repertory Theater, 15 West 28th Street, New York, NY 10001, on October 4th, 1994.

Director: ....Saundra McClain
Set Designer: ....Watoku Ueno
Lighting Designer: ....Greg MacPherson
Costume Designer:..Carol Ann Pelletier

CAST, IN ORDER OF APPEARANCE

Aimée..Elizabeth Perry
Raymond..Fred Burrell
Cristelle ....Melissa Chalsma
Marie-Jo.. Elizabeth Hess
Modeste ....Abdoulaye N'Gom

Produced by Ubu Repertory Theater
Françoise Kourilsky, *Artistic Director*

CHARACTERS

RAYMOND, *the Grandfather*

AIMEE, *the Grandmother*

CRISTELLE, *their Granddaughter*

MARIE-JO, *their Daughter, mother of Cristelle*

MODESTE, *a native of Ivory Coast, the Servant*

SETTING

The action takes place during the course of three days; the scene is the kitchen-dining area, a room in a fair degree of disorder and quite unlike the photographs of its counterparts one might see in such magazines as "House and Gardens." Nothing is new; nothing matches. The dining room furniture is heavy and too large for the space. The table and the top of the buffet are covered with piles of newspapers, a sewing kit, sewing machine, fabrics, fruits and vegetables. The furniture looks secondhand, as does the refrigerator; the room has a thrown-together look (there are electric cords and extensions strung up haphazardly around the room), and here and there the linoleum has come unglued. The same is true of the wall paper, which, although consistently in yellow and beige, is a different pattern on each wall.

In one corner of the room, by a radiator, stands a large dog's basket filled with doggie toys, but there is no dog. Above the basket hangs a small corner whatnot on which stands a large framed photograph of a powerful boxer dog, taken head on, and a small vase containing artificial flowers. Shelves stage left hold a few books, a record player, records and more photographs. Two bad paintings hang on the walls, one representing a small fishing village and the other a view of autumn woods; there is also a painted plate with the portrait of General de Gaulle.

On the back wall sliding glass doors give onto a small modern porch with plants, a garden table and brown recliner. Beyond is a darkish cement courtyard, which is surrounded by a high gray wall.

DAY ONE

The curtain rises on daylight. Fine summer weather.
Near the radiator between the window and the dog's basket a
woman in her fifties (Aimée) is sitting under a hair dryer which
is humming noisily. She is wearing a dressing gown with large
pink and purple flowers and brown sandals. She wears glasses
and is looking through a department-store advertising supple-
ment while glancing from time to time out of the window (the
glances vary in length according to what she happens to see).
After a moment the door stage right opens and a man in his early
sixties (Raymond) enters. He is wearing beige shorts, a white
sleeveless T-shirt and sandals. He opens one of the doors in the
buffet and takes out a bowl, which he sets on the table. His wife
watches him. She speaks in a loud voice because of the noise from
her hair dryer.

AIMEE: Well look at you — you must think you're in Saint-Tropez.
(*He goes to the sink and gets a spoon, a knife and a dishcloth. His wife
is now looking out of the window.*) There she goes again, in and out.
Some people sure seem to know how to waste time.

RAYMOND: Who's that?

Wiping the knife and spoon, he moves to the window.

AIMEE: Get a load of that, will you? — for people who're out of
work, they sure manage to take care of themselves...

RAYMOND: She looks like she's got on her little sister's skirt, you
can almost see her pussy.

AIMEE: Will you look at that skirt, what a tramp!

RAYMOND: It's unbelievable, just look at her — and people are
surprised at the number of rapes... Is that the new supermarket
catalogue?

AIMEE: Ah, they're having a sale on wine.

1

She hands him the supplement, he takes it to the table and sits down, stage left, turning his back on his wife. He puts down the dishtowel, the utensils and the supplement. The opposite end of the table is covered with a sewing machine and a pile of fabrics. Next to them are piles of magazines like "House and Gardens", "Jours de France", "Ici Paris", "France-Dimanche", "Detective", etc., a basket of fruit, some vegetables, a sugar bowl, a butter dish and a thermos bottle, which he picks up and opens to pour out some coffee.

RAYMOND: Is this all the coffee that's left? I'm talking to you...

He is holding the supplement.

AIMEE: What do you think about the wine?

RAYMOND: I'm asking about the coffee.

AIMEE: What?

She takes her head out of the dryer.

RAYMOND: Have you gone deaf or what?

AIMEE: Don't be silly, you can see I'm under the dryer. What did you say?

RAYMOND: Coffee.

AIMEE: Blame your sister-in-law.

RAYMOND: Which one?

AIMEE: Jeanne Personnic.

RAYMOND: There's no more bread.

AIMEE: There are some of your salt-free crackers.

She goes back under the dryer and picks up "France-Dimanche," which she has on her lap.

RAYMOND: I kept the end of the baguette from last night.

He rises and gets a package of rusks from the refrigerator and puts it on the table, goes to the buffet and rummages around for something amid the clutter on the top—ironed clothes, clean dishes, iron, letters, bottles, hair brush, framed photographs, etc.

AIMEE: If you're looking for your medicine, it's there in the rotis-somat. (*He turns to his wife, then goes to the refrigerator, on which sits the aforementioned rotissomat—neither overly new nor clean.*) Well, we don't use it in the summertime since we've got the barbecue. This way you'll have it in easy reach. Whew, it's hot! While you're up, would you open the sliding doors and the door to the stairs, that should pull some air in.

RAYMOND: You could do it yourself.

AIMEE: Don't forget your digitalis today. It's the most important.

RAYMOND: Screw it.

He sets the medicines on the table and goes to the sink, gets a glass of water and returns to sit down at his place. He swallows two capsules and begins dripping the digitalis into his glass.

AIMEE: Fifteen drops, no more, Guiguitte says it's dangerous stuff.

RAYMOND: I can count. (*He drinks down the glass of water, rises, goes to the sink, rinses out the glass and drinks some more water.*) It tastes bitter.

AIMEE: The door. (*Raymond turns to her.*) I'm under the dryer.

RAYMOND: I don't see your ass glued to the chair.

He opens the door stage right and the sliding doors to the porch, returns to his seat and begins to butter a rusk.

AIMEE: It's really strange, Catherine Deneuve, you never see her with a man that one, and yet she's really very pretty. Of course you don't see her smiling a lot so maybe she's not much fun, kind of frigid. (*She removes her head from the dryer, rises and unplugs it.*) Whew! It's hot. I'm all damp.

RAYMOND: She's not the only one who's frigid.

AIMEE: Who?

RAYMOND: Catherine Deneuve.

AIMEE: Why do you say that?

RAYMOND: I just do.

AIMEE: Okay, don't start in on that again. You were all over me last night, I was too hot, I didn't get a wink of sleep.

RAYMOND: You promised.

She returns her chair to the table and begins removing her curlers, which she places in a plastic box on the buffet; she puts "France-Dimanche" on the table in front of her husband.

AIMEE: I didn't promise you a thing.

RAYMOND: You've got a short memory.

AIMEE: Listen, Raymond, you've got to get it through your head that I'm not interested in that kind of thing any more.

RAYMOND: I might as well just cut it off, I guess.

AIMEE: Sometimes you can really be dense. I've already told you: from now on we're just going to be pals.

RAYMOND: Pals — now I've heard everything!

AIMEE: Well, that's the way it is. We're not going to keep on arguing about it. I think I can afford to treat myself to a permanent. I'll go next week with Marie-Jo.

RAYMOND: What are you going to use for money?

AIMEE: I'm not asking you for any — I've got some put away.

RAYMOND: I thought you'd spent all that.

AIMEE: When I made those curtains for the Le Gloans I gave you 350 francs and I kept 150 for my hair.

RAYMOND: What did my sister-in-law want?

AIMEE: To borrow your ladder to repaint her kitchen.

RAYMOND: You didn't let her have it, I hope?

AIMEE: You think I'm crazy? Of course not! She only comes when she wants something.

RAYMOND: She's the one who ate my bread.

AIMEE: That, I couldn't say no.

> *She has removed her curlers and now begins to brush out her hair with the brush she takes from the buffet, standing next to the dog's basket and using the sliding doors as a mirror.*

RAYMOND: They've got some 12-year-old whiskey for 60 francs.

AIMEE: You can't have it: diet. You know what the doctor said.

RAYMOND: I don't give a shit.

AIMEE: Well, I do. I'm not going to end up here in this stinking hole with only half your pension.

RAYMOND: You'll go to Bob and Marie-Jo.

AIMEE: Can you imagine me surrounded by a pack of zulus? I'd rather be dead, I can tell you that.

She has finished doing her hair and puts the brush down on the table, then goes to the sink where she washes the two bowls and the tableware. Raymond picks up the "France-Dimanche" she has put on the table and begins to look at it while eating a second rusk. A long silence. Aimée puts the cover on the sewing machine and puts it behind the dog's basket and then gathers up the pieces of fabric and takes them out to the garden table on the porch.

AIMEE: It's like a steam bath. You didn't open the porch door. (*She does so. The sounds of birds chirping; these sounds will continue to the end of the scene.*) Marie-Jo will feel right at home, with all this heat. The radio said that it hadn't been this hot since 1882. Well I'll be...I can't believe what I'm seeing!

She goes to the window and looks out, holding the curtain aside.

RAYMOND: What.

AIMEE: The dog that belongs to the fish store is doing it with the one from next door.

RAYMOND: So?

AIMEE: They're both males, for Chrissake.

RAYMOND: So, one of them must be a fag.

AIMEE: Well, if dogs are starting in with that, we've had it. Poor old fella, he's really getting it good.

RAYMOND: Patrick Duffy is giving up everything for Mireille Mathieu.

AIMEE: Who's he?

RAYMOND: Bobby, on "Dallas."

AIMEE: Show me, I must have skipped a page. (*She comes over to her husband and starts reading over his shoulder.*) She looks like a real dummy. Isn't he supposed to be married, that one?

RAYMOND: I don't know.

AIMEE: I think he is. Actors are peculiar...

> *A girl of 16 (Cristelle) enters from the door stage right. She is wearing a long white T-shirt which comes down mid-thigh and is barefoot. She is barely awake.*

AIMEE: Good morning.

CRISTELLE: 'Morning.

AIMEE: Good morning my little pet.

> *Cristelle kisses Aimée and Raymond.*

RAYMOND: There's no more coffee.

AIMEE: I'll make some for you, my sweets.

RAYMOND: Oh, thanks a lot!

> *Aimée moves to the sink, Cristelle goes to the refrigerator and opens it. She takes out a large bottle of Coca-Cola, takes a glass from the sink and sits down across from Raymond.*

AIMEE: Don't you want any coffee?

CRISTELLE: No.

RAYMOND: Will you get a load of that, drinking that garbage for breakfast...

AIMEE: So what, if it's what she likes.

She begins to straighten the things lying on the top of the buffet.

RAYMOND: Aren't you going to make coffee?

AIMEE: She doesn't want any.

RAYMOND: What about me?

AIMEE: It gives you palpitations.

RAYMOND: Palpitations.

AIMEE: That's what the doctor said.

RAYMOND: The doctor.

AIMEE: Are you finished repeating everything I say?

RAYMOND: There's no more bread.

AIMEE: You could give her one of your crackers. (*She comes to the table, takes the package of rusks and sets it in front of Cristelle.*) You can be so selfish...

CRISTELLE: Don't start in on my account, I'm not hungry.

AIMEE: See what you've done?

RAYMOND: I didn't do anything.

AIMEE: Oh no? And you're going to eat something for me, I don't want your mother saying we haven't fed you.

She opens one of the doors of the buffet, crouches down, rummages around inside and brings out an unopened jar of jam, which she puts on the table.

RAYMOND: Where did the jam come from?

AIMEE: You saw me, from the buffet.

RAYMOND: I thought we didn't have any more.

AIMEE: Well, as you can see, we do.

CRISTELLE: I can't get it open.

AIMEE: Ask your grandfather.

RAYMOND: Well, at least I'm good for something.

AIMEE: Okay, don't get your pants in an uproar.

He unscrews the lid; she takes some window-cleaner from under the sink and a rag and goes to the sliding door, where she was brushing her hair. She begins to polish the glass.

AIMEE: Your niece is getting married.

RAYMOND: Which one?

AIMEE: Your sister's girl.

RAYMOND: Who told you so?

AIMEE: Your sister-in-law.

RAYMOND: How did she know?

AIMEE: Your sister.

RAYMOND: I saw her yesterday, she didn't say anything to me.

AIMEE: Of course she didn't. We don't count. As a matter of fact, I might as well say it right out: We're less than nothing. But when we lived in Paris, oh yes, it was different then, then it was "Auntie" this and "Unkie" that, day in day out.

RAYMOND: They didn't know any place to go.

AIMEE: That's what I'm saying—they knew where *we* lived. It's like your nephew, he only got to be a cop thanks to you.

RAYMOND: You can say that again. We're going to have to buy a wedding present.

AIMEE: There, I draw the line. I never liked that kid.

CRISTELLE: Which one is she?

AIMEE: Françoise.

CRISTELLE: She's a dope.

AIMEE: See? (*Cristelle gets up and moves to the recliner on the porch, carrying her rusk and glass of coke.*) You're going to be too hot. What did you do last night?

CRISTELLE: I went down to the cafe with the gang.

AIMEE: Did you get home late?

CRISTELLE: Eleven-thirty.

RAYMOND: Come on... — it was one o'clock.

CRISTELLE: That's not true.

RAYMOND: I turned off the TV at ten past twelve. All that's going to change when your mother gets here...

CRISTELLE: I don't give a shit.

10

RAYMOND: She doesn't like you going out.

AIMEE: You're really something! You were sixteen once, and so was I. Youth must be served, as they say.

RAYMOND: Sure, but in *my* day...

AIMEE: All right, just hold it right there. First, your day is done and gone.

RAYMOND: I'm still around, as far as I know.

AIMEE: You won't be for much longer, if you keep on like that. If you think I didn't see you taking the jam...you're worse than a kid.

RAYMOND: What do you think we're living on?

AIMEE: Your pension, and don't I know it! If you'd only worked ten more years, we wouldn't be in this fix.

RAYMOND: You weren't the one who was working your ass off.

AIMEE: Oh, I know, I've never done anything.

CRISTELLE: You're worse than my folks: bicker, bicker, bicker.

AIMEE: Your mother is not an easy woman.

RAYMOND: Like mother, like daughter.

AIMEE: Like father, like daughter, you mean. She's got your temper. (*The telephone rings.*) That'll be Guiguitte. (*She answers it.*) Hello? It's not true! Well, talk about long-lost friends! Surprise, this is a surprise! Well, how are you? Fine... Yes... Oh... Oh sure... Well, so much the better... Of course... You'd better believe it... Fine... Fine... Fine... I'm so glad for you... Fine... And what about Jacques? Yes... Fine... Fine... Poor guy... It'll do him good... And your mother? Go on... No kidding... Whew!... She must have had

11

a scare!... In her shoes... You'd better believe it... No, in broad daylight... Stop it, you're giving me the shivers... Oh, la la... If she'd come when they were still there... And what about her cats? Oh yes?... And your dog? Oh yes... You know we lost ours... Yes....two months ago, it was prostate cancer... Yes... No, not all that old, eleven... He was so brave. But I know he suffered. The vet operated on him in February, for a couple of months it was a little better, and then in April it all of a sudden got worse. He went very quick. It really threw us for a loop, not that things had been going all that well before...

RAYMOND: There you are, she's off and running!

AIMEE: What can I say, I'm bored as-they-say shitless here, you'll pardon the expression. It's so dead here, nothing ever happens.

RAYMOND: Bitch bitch bitch...

AIMEE: Luckily I've got my cousin Guiguitte, I go out with her. You'll laugh, but I even go with her when she goes to funerals, it gets me out of the house. Raymond calls us Our Ladies of the Cemetery. People here are really nasty, everybody into everybody else's business...

RAYMOND: Starting with you.

AIMEE: Can you keep it down — can't you see I'm talking? It's my husband carrying on. He's fine. Fanny says hello.

RAYMOND: Ah...

AIMEE: Him too... The latest tests weren't any better and they weren't any worse. What can you do, he won't stick to his diet, any old excuse will do...

RAYMOND: I'd like to see you stick to it.

AIMEE: You heard him. Why don't you start stringing those beans?

12

You there, help your grandfather. Use the basin under the sink.

Cristelle gets up, takes the basin and sits down across from Raymond. They begin to string beans.

AIMEE: (*still speaking into the telephone*) That's Cristelle. We've had her since February. You didn't know? How long has it been since we talked?

RAYMOND: They'll be at it for hours, that one can really shoot the breeze...

AIMEE: That long... She's been here for over five months... No, it's summer vacation now, otherwise she boards with the sisters and we have her on weekends... It was love... That's right, at her age... Like mother, like daughter...

CRISTELLE: She's not going to start in on my life story is she...

RAYMOND: Try and stop her.

AIMEE: Well, no one knows for sure...more like a crush.

CRISTELLE: Grandma, that's enough!

AIMEE: Yes, but it was with some African kid, the prefect's son. You know Marie-Jo, she's got her head screwed on right, she packed her off to us right away.

CRISTELLE: Grandma, can't you just shut up and mind your own business...shit!

AIMEE: And what about you...

CRISTELLE: She's always criticizing other people, but she's just as bad.

AIMEE: Is that right? Where? In the Chevreuse is it!? How many rooms? That's incredible!

RAYMOND: Are you glad?

CRISTELLE: Why?

RAYMOND: To be seeing your mother?

CRISTELLE: What do you think?

AIMEE: (*on the telephone*) Yes. She's getting in today, as a matter of fact. It's been two years since they were here. Her husband's not coming until after the fourteenth of July... What's your weather been like? No air at all. We're sweating... That's what I was telling Raymond.

RAYMOND: What did I say now?

AIMEE: Cristelle, Karim's going by.

Cristelle dashes to the window and then returns to the table.

CRISTELLE: I missed him.

AIMEE: He was on his motorcycle. Yes, I'm listening. You'd better believe it...

RAYMOND: Who's this Karim?

CRISTELLE: Jeanne Bonniec's son.

RAYMOND: With a name like that?

CRISTELLE: You really make me sick when you say things like that.

RAYMOND: Like what?

CRISTELLE: Nothing.

AIMEE: (*on the telephone*) Of course I'm interested, it'll add a

14

little to the kitty... When? Perfect...

RAYMOND: You'd better not tell your mother that we've been letting you stay out on Saturdays.

CRISTELLE: I'm not stupid.

AIMEE: I'll have to talk to you-know-who, if you know what I mean...

RAYMOND: Okay, okay, what's she going to ask for now?

AIMEE: Oh, the lucky things. Me too, especially since I haven't done much this morning. I must admit I'm still in my robe... No, noon... No, she'll take a cab... Twenty kilometers... What can you do, there's not even a train station in this Godforsaken hole, and as for shopping, don't even ask... We get to the mall once a week with my cousin... She's fine. The children have all turned out well, she's got money. It's a good thing she's here, she's easy to get along with. Okay, I'll leave you, it's been great to hear your voice, give Jacques and your mother a kiss for me... Yes, fine, very soon. 'Bye. (*She hangs up and goes back to cleaning the window.*) That was Fanny.

RAYMOND: We gathered that.

CRISTELLE: How come you were telling her about me?

AIMEE: Oh, she's no problem, she's very broadminded.

CRISTELLE: I don't like people talking —

AIMEE: She understands. When she was eighteen, she had a crush on a Chinese student.

RAYMOND: He was from Indochina.

AIMEE: Why not make it Cochin China, while you're at it?

15

RAYMOND: As a matter of fact, he was Cambodian.

AIMEE: Okay, we get the picture. All the same, she stuck by him, and Lord knows her family was against it... Of course, it was like that with me and your father in the beginning. Still, they've been married now for twenty years, Jacques has a very good job.

CRISTELLE: Jacques doesn't sound very Chinese.

AIMEE: He was born in France.

RAYMOND: Do you know how long you were on the phone?

AIMEE: You weren't paying.

RAYMOND: For once.

AIMEE: Okay, you can hold it right there — you can't say I use the phone a lot, excepting to call Guiguitte. (*The telephone rings.*) Well, I guess it's one of those days. (*She answers.*) Hello... Well, speak of the Devil! You've been trying? I was talking to Fanny, my friend in Paris. They've just bought a nine-room house, she wants me to make all the curtains... More than three million, with a big garden. Imagine! Everybody I know is well off, if I do say so myself. (*She suddenly stares through the window.*) I can't believe my eyes — I must be dreaming. It's Marie-Jo!

RAYMOND: What are you talking about?

AIMEE: She's right there, I can see her, getting out of a cab. (*Cristelle rises and runs out the door, stage left. Raymond goes to the window.*) Yes, I've got to hang up... No, I can't ask you to come around for lunch, I've only got four steaks. Come by for coffee. Marie-Jo will be glad to see you. Fine, see you then! (*She hangs up and goes to the window.*) She must have caught an earlier train.

RAYMOND: Who's the ape man?

AIMEE: How should I know? So, what are you standing there for, go give him a hand. (*He exits stage right, Aimée continues to watch from the window.*) Cristelle, you mother's here! I'll finish that later...

> *She moves to put away the cleaning products and rag beneath the sink. A woman of thirty-five (Marie-Jo) enters. She is wearing light cotton slacks and a sleeveless T-shirt. She carries a vanity case, a carry-on case and a plastic bag marked "Duty Free Shop". She sets them on a corner of the table.*

AIMEE: I didn't expect you so early.

MARIE-JO: That's Air Africa for you! What a flight!

AIMEE: Hello.

> *They embrace. Raymond enters carrying two very heavy suitcases, which he sets down by the dog's basket.*

RAYMOND: What have you got in here, elephant tusks?

MARIE-JO: I brought my silverware back, it's safer.

AIMEE: You're looking good.

MARIE-JO: I'm holding my own. What's *he* up to? Come on in. They're not going to eat you, you big dummy.

AIMEE: Who's this?

MARIE-JO: My boy.

> *An African man, thirty-five years old, enters, carrying two suitcases and a large carry-on bag. This is Modeste. He is wearing a pale green pantsuit with a dark red V-neck sweater and white shirt. He is wearing tennis shoes.*

MARIE-JO: This is Modeste...this is my mother.

MODESTE: How do you do, Ma'am.

AIMEE: Hello. If I'd known...

MARIE-JO: And where's the kid, still in the sack?

AIMEE: She was here a minute ago, she was up at the crack of dawn, really, she's so happy...

MARIE-JO: How's it been going?

AIMEE: Fine, she's no trouble at all.

MARIE-JO: You don't say.

RAYMOND: You can put those suitcases down here, fella, you'll be more comfortable.

MODESTE: Thank you, sir.

> *Modeste goes to stand by the dog's basket. Cristelle enters. She is wearing jeans and a freshly ironed white shirt with short sleeves.*

CRISTELLE: Modeste! I don't believe it!

> *She runs to him and kisses him. He takes a cassette from his pocket and gives it to her.*

MODESTE: Here.

CRISTELLE: Alpha Blondy, cool!

AIMEE: And what about your mother?

CRISTELLE: Hi.

RAYMOND: Really!

Cristelle goes to her mother and kisses her.

MARIE-JO: Hi. Grown, hasn't she?

RAYMOND: Well, she sure eats enough.

AIMEE: Oh yes, when it comes to eating, she eats. As a matter of fact, she's a real bottomless pit.

MARIE-JO: I'm so thirsty... How about a beer?

AIMEE: Your father bought some yesterday.

> *Aimée goes to the refrigerator, takes out a beer, takes a glass from the sink and serves her daughter.*

MARIE-JO: What about you, Modeste? Aren't you thirsty?

MODESTE: No, Ma'am, thank you.

MARIE-JO: He's never thirsty...a real camel, aren't you, Modeste?

MODESTE: Yes, Ma'am.

MARIE-JO: You can start taking my suitcases up to my room. Cristelle, show him the way. (*Cristelle and Modeste take all the suitcases. To Modeste*) Leave yours here, we'll see to it later.

CRISTELLE: (*to Modeste*) I'm glad to see you.

> *They exit.*

AIMEE: Look out for the wallpaper on the stairs, I've just put up new! So now, out with it...what's all this about?

RAYMOND: You might have warned us.

MARIE-JO: I can go somewhere else if I'm putting you out.

AIMEE: That's not it — but you might have warned us, as your father says.

MARIE-JO: It all happened so quick, Bob and I decided to buy Doctor Callarec's house...

RAYMOND: No kidding.

AIMEE: How much?

MARIE-JO: Seventy.

RAYMOND: You're coming back to France?

MARIE-JO: Later. Like Bob says, we've got to put our money into something — "You never can tell."

AIMEE: Some people are going to be jealous...

MARIE-JO: Who?

AIMEE: (*indicating Raymond*) His folks.

RAYMOND: Tough shit!

MARIE-JO: There's a lot of work to be done, that's why I brought Modeste along. He's a good worker, and he's well-behaved. And it's a bargain, the company's paying his fare.

AIMEE: Fine, but where are we going to put him?

MARIE-JO: He can bed down anywhere. We could put him in the next room.

RAYMOND: What about my TV?

MARIE-JO: Don't worry, he'll wait until you go to bed, he's used to it. But he's reliable, not a thief, and he's clean.

AIMEE: Yes, but where will we put the kid when Bob gets here?

MARIE-JO: We can think about that when the time comes...right now, I need a shower.

AIMEE: I'm going to get dressed. Your father will show you about the water heater, it's a little temperamental. Are you coming, Raymond?

> *They exit, stage right.*

AIMEE: (*offstage*) See the new wall paper? It's brighter, don't you think?

MARIE-JO: (*offstage*) Lots.

AIMEE: (*offstage*) I hung it myself.

MARIE-JO: (*offstage*) I've got to call Bob.

AIMEE: (*offstage*) Maybe we could go to the mall this afternoon, with Guiguitte.

> *The stage is now empty. The curtain falls slowly, to the music of Alpha Blondy singing "Interplanetary Revolution."*

DAY TWO

Afternoon. The weather is still hot and sunny, the sun is shining in through the sliding doors. Lunch is over; Raymond is still sitting where he sat for breakfast on Day One. He is wearing a pair of beige cloth trousers and a white shirt (he has an African charm hanging around his neck). Marie-Jo sits on his right; she is wearing a pink gingham dress with short sleeves and round neckline. Aimée, sitting across from Raymond, is wearing a sleeveless rayon print dress with violet flowers and an imitation ivory bracelet on her right wrist. Cristelle, who is seated next to her, is wearing the same jeans as the day before and a T-shirt with a picture of the Ivory Coast singer Alpha Blondy. To Cristelle's left there is a place for Modeste. The table has been partially cleared; the adults are drinking coffee, Cristelle's plate, half-full, is still in front of her. Modeste, wearing jeans, a white T-shirt and a blue apron tied around his waist, is standing at the sink. He is washing the dishes.

MARIE-JO: You haven't done all that well for someone who's supposed to have such a great appetite.

CRISTELLE: I'm not hungry.

MARIE-JO: You'll eat what's in front of you.

CRISTELLE: I've got a headache, I'm expecting my period.

RAYMOND: We're at the table, do you mind?

CRISTELLE: It's true.

MARIE-JO: That'll be enough of that, okay? Just snap out of it!

RAYMOND: Give it to me, I'll finish it.

AIMEE: I was waiting for that.

MARIE-JO: She'll eat it. Is this how you show your appreciation for Modeste's cooking?

AIMEE: That's right, and especially since it was good. Thank you, Modeste. Who taught you to cook?

MODESTE: Ma'am did.

MARIE-JO: Except for African food. Eat, or I'm going to let you have it.

Cristelle begins to eat very slowly.

AIMEE: Some day you'll have to make me something African.

CRISTELLE: Icky bananas and agoutis.

RAYMOND: What's an agouti?

CRISTELLE: The agouti's like a big rat.

AIMEE: How disgusting.

CRISTELLE: Or maybe snake or monkey.

AIMEE: Stop!

MARIE-JO: Snake can be quite good — the rest is disgusting.

AIMEE: Snake...just the thought of it makes me want to puke.

RAYMOND: In Indochina we ate rotten eggs.

AIMEE: That really takes the cake...

RAYMOND: You might say that...

AIMEE: If you've told me once, you've told me a hundred

times. Right now, we're in France, so we'll eat French. Isn't that right, Modeste?

MODESTE: Yes, Ma'am.

AIMEE: I can't tell you how much I like my bracelet, Modeste. It's lovely.

MODESTE: Thank you, Ma'am.

RAYMOND: Where did you get this coffee?

AIMEE: Marie-Jo bought it yesterday at the supermarket. Why?

RAYMOND: It's not bad.

AIMEE: I should think so...it's pure Arabica.

MARIE-JO: Is that you in the picture?

AIMEE: The one on the buffet? No, that's Guiguitte.

MARIE-JO: It's funny, sometimes you look alike.

AIMEE: Why do you think your father married me?

RAYMOND: Of course, if I'd married *her* I'd be better off today.

AIMEE: She'd had to have said yes, of course.

RAYMOND: Let's run through that again, shall we...?

AIMEE: What? Oh, all right — everybody knows you've got your high-school diploma.

MARIE-JO: Well, I see things haven't changed much around here.

AIMEE: What do you want, we're too old to change.

RAYMOND: If I had it to do over again, you can believe...

AIMEE: And what about me? Let me give you a piece of advice, Modeste: Don't get married.

MARIE-JO: It's too late for that, he's got seven kids. Isn't that right?

MODESTE: Yes, Ma'am.

AIMEE: Don't you have any consideration for your poor wife?

RAYMOND: My mother had seven kids too.

AIMEE: Exactly, and it killed her, the poor woman.

MARIE-JO: Stop drinking so much coke, I can't stand it... In Africa all she'd drink was water.

AIMEE: Speaking of water, I've got something to show you. (*She rises, goes to the buffet, opens the upper cupboard, takes something out and returns to her chair. She hands Marie-Jo a small, clear-glass pharmaceutical bottle, which is apparently empty.*) There.

MARIE-JO: What is it?

RAYMOND: Look.

MARIE-JO: I don't see anything.

AIMEE: Well, that beats all! Put on your glasses.

MARIE-JO: That little thing? What is it?

CRISTELLE: It's one of grandma's boogers.

MARIE-JO: Silly! What is it?

AIMEE: Can't you guess? It's my stone.

25

MARIE-JO: That small?

AIMEE: I'd like to have seen you put up with it.

She rises and replaces the bottle in the cupboard and then removes the coffee cups and places them in the sink, where Modeste is still standing.

CRISTELLE: *Mité*, Modeste.

MODESTE: *Tigba loffi plé.*

CRISTELLE: *Nansioh.*

MODESTE: *Mi nan pan.**

AIMEE: Now you're talking African?

CRISTELLE: It's Senufu.

AIMEE: You could have fooled me...

MARIE-JO: She'd do better to speak English.

RAYMOND: Say something else.

CRISTELLE: *Yola.*

AIMEE: What does that mean?

CRISTELLE: I don't feel like talking.

AIMEE: In my day, we didn't learn those kinds of languages.

*Translation of the dialogue:
        CRISTELLE: Modeste, I can't stand it any more.
        MODESTE: Be brave, little white girl.
        CRISTELLE: Save me.
        MODESTE: I will.

RAYMOND: The other day I heard some French singer singing *La vie en rose* in Japanese.

AIMEE: Edith Piaf.

RAYMOND: No, this one was alive.

AIMEE: Oh yes?

The telephone rings. Marie-Jo gets up to answer it.

MARIE-JO: That'll be Bob.

RAYMOND: Or Guiguitte.

AIMEE: No, it's not her time.

Modeste goes to the table, takes Cristelle's plate and returns to the sink. Marie-Jo picks up the phone.

MARIE-JO: Hello? Hello? Here we go... Modeste, I saw that! Hello? Yes, I'm here, it's me. Can you hear me? He can't hear me.

RAYMOND: Can you hear him?

MARIE-JO: Sure, he's yelling at the top of his voice. Hello? Hello? What a crock — Africa in all its shitty splendor.

RAYMOND: It's the same when you call us.

MARIE-JO: It's the switchboard in Katiola...the lazy slugs. They're not what you'd call hard workers, right Modeste?

MODESTE: Yes, Ma'am.

MARIE-JO: A really crappy country! Hello? This could go on for hours. They don't know how to make *any*thing work — if your fridge breaks down, you just toss it out.

AIMEE: That must make things difficult...

MARIE-JO: Well, finally! I've been trying to get you since yesterday. What? There's some kind of crackling sound... It was awful, we couldn't land at Ouaga because of the curfew. Exhausting, the food was vile... He's fine. Modeste, the Mister wants to know if you're happy? He wants to know what you think of the women in Brittany. (*Modeste smiles.*) Nothing. He's laughing.

AIMEE: You want to be careful, Modeste, they can get you into trouble.

RAYMOND: We'll have to send him out to see the Le Du sisters.

AIMEE: That's an awful thing to say, what a dirty mind!

CRISTELLE: Who're they?

AIMEE: Those two sluts who have that bar on the road to Trégrom...they say that all kinds of things go on out there.

MARIE-JO: Mother, could you keep it down, it's hard enough to hear as it is... Yes. Your father wants to know how's his baby girl?

CRISTELLE: Tell him to bring me a Walkman.

RAYMOND: They say those things make you deaf.

CRISTELLE: Like masturbation.

AIMEE: Honey-bun...

MARIE-JO: Will you shut up, Mother! Wait, don't hang up. I can't manage this, Cristelle, give me a hand.

Marie-Jo takes the telephone, Cristelle opens the door, stage right.

CRISTELLE: A Walkman.

MARIE-JO: Can you hear her? Forget it.

She exits, carrying the telephone. Cristelle shuts the door behind her and goes to sit in the recliner on the porch.

CRISTELLE: She's a real pain, the bitch.

AIMEE: Honey-bun...

CRISTELLE: It's true, she won't even let me talk to him. She's jealous, she's always on my case. She still thinks I'm ten years old.

RAYMOND: Is that how we talk about our mothers these days? The times we live in!

AIMEE: Well, now, let me stop you right there — Marie-Jo wasn't more than thirteen when she called me a bitch and a slut right in the middle of the dime store at the Place d'Italie.

Modeste has finished the dishes; he takes a sponge from the sink and wipes off the table. Raymond and Aimée fold their napkins.

AIMEE: I told the fish man that his dog was a fag...

RAYMOND: What did he say?

AIMEE: Nothing. He laughed.

The door stage right opens. Marie-Jo appears with the telephone. She is still holding the receiver to her ear and has not finished talking.

MARIE-JO: Modeste, what's your cousin's name who has a wife in Yamoussukro?

MODESTE: Koffi.

Marie-Jo exits.

MARIE-JO: *(from offstage)* Not Mita, he's a dope — he's illiterate, and he's dirty to boot.

RAYMOND: Listen to those names, can you believe it!

AIMEE: You think "Camfrout" or "Plounéour-Ménez" are any better?

MARIE-JO: *(from offstage)* Mother, get the door!

> *Aimée rises and shuts the door.*

AIMEE: You'd think I was her slave.

RAYMOND: So, fella, how's it going?

MODESTE: Fine, Sir.

RAYMOND: You've sure got a heavy hand with the soap.

AIMEE: Let me see... Well, you certainly don't do anything by halves, do you... Here, I'll show you...

RAYMOND: Fine, I'm going to watch TV.

AIMEE: Okay.

> *Raymond rises and exits, stage right. We glimpse Marie-Jo, still on the telephone. Aimée and Modeste are at the sink.*

AIMEE: First, you rinse out the sponge real good... Like this. You could clean the whole kitchen with the amount of soap you used... (*As she speaks, she makes broad gestures to indicate the entire room and pronounces each word and syllable very distinctly.*) See, all you need is a little drop.

CRISTELLE: Grandma, lay off. He's not retarded.

MODESTE: *Loffi pili pé ba yé bai ka.*

CRISTELLE: (*laughing*) With tomato sauce.

AIMEE: What did he say?

CRISTELLE: "White folks, someday you're going to get eaten."

AIMEE: That's not funny.

CRISTELLE: It's the title of a book.

AIMEE: All the same...I guess that's what you call black humor, but it's still not funny.

CRISTELLE: It was written by a white man.

AIMEE: Well, there are fools the world over. What are you waiting for, you're not going to leave all that soap on the table are you?

> *Modeste returns to the table, Aimée picks up the bottle of Coca-Cola and moves to the refrigerator.*

CRISTELLE: I'm thirsty.

AIMEE: Well, quick then, before Miss Complainer comes back. (*She goes to the buffet, takes a glass, pours some Coca-Cola and takes it to Cristelle.*) You're going to roast, my darling.

CRISTELLE: Medium rare, for Modeste.

AIMEE: He must feel right at home, as a matter of fact, with all this heat...

CRISTELLE: This is nothing, it's more than twice what it is here.

AIMEE: How awful, I'd be dead already. It's already stifling here...in fact, I'm about to melt.

> *Cristelle drains her glass and hands it back to Aimée, who puts it in the sink and then replaces the bottle of Coca-Cola in the*

refrigerator. Modeste has finished cleaning the table. He returns to the sink and rinses out the sponge.

AIMEE: There's another glass there... That one sure can talk, can't she — what has she got, acute telephonitis or something?

CRISTELLE: That's how they always are when they don't have to pay.

AIMEE: You took the words right out of my mouth.

CRISTELLE: Papa calls his mother every day.

AIMEE: I know, every time I run into her it's: "The children called, everything's fine..." She gets on my nerves, with her sweety voice. What can I say, she's just a hick.

CRISTELLE: She's nice...

AIMEE: It depends on who you... Well, poor woman, I'll say nothing. Come here, Modeste, I'm going to show you about the clothes.

MODESTE: Yes, Ma'am.

Marie-Jo enters carrying the telephone, which she returns to its place.

MARIE-JO: Modeste, Mamadou has had an accident, he was knocked down by a car on the road to Bouaké.

MODESTE: Is he dead?

MARIE-JO: No, but he might as well be. Bob thinks he's had it.

AIMEE: Who's that?

MARIE-JO: Our super.

AIMEE: Poor fellow.

MARIE-JO: I was right to bring my silverware. Is he reliable, this Koffi?

MODESTE: Yes, Ma'am.

MARIE-JO: I hope so. I'd better get changed to go to the lawyer's. Do you want to come along?

AIMEE: I wouldn't say no, I've never been to their place. They say they've got some nice things.

MARIE-JO: Modeste, you can take care of the washing.

AIMEE: I was just going to show him... Come along.

Aimée and Modeste exit by the porch.

MARIE-JO: Are you going to spend the rest of your life lying there! Get a move on.

CRISTELLE: I'm bored.

MARIE-JO: I'll give you bored. When I was your age there was always plenty to do.

CRISTELLE: What?

MARIE-JO: I don't know, different things. When I get back from the lawyer's we'll go see your Aunt Renée.

CRISTELLE: I'm thrilled.

MARIE-JO: Who's that wog that keeps driving by on the motorbike?

CRISTELLE: I don't know, I'm not grandma, I don't spend all my time at the window.

MARIE-JO: You must really think I'm an idiot... If you think I'm not on to your little tricks...he keeps looking over here.

33

CRISTELLE: It's a public street.

MARIE-JO: I'm warning you, you'd better not start that kind of thing again...

CRISTELLE: I haven't done anything.

MARIE-JO: Just for beginners, you'll do me the favor of taking off that T-shirt. I don't want you going out in that.

CRISTELLE: It's Alpha Blondy.

MARIE-JO: I can read. We're not in Africa.

CRISTELLE: Disgusting.

MARIE-JO: What did you say?

CRISTELLE: Nothing.

MARIE-JO: You'll see when your father gets here.

CRISTELLE: If I'm not dead first.

MARIE-JO: Right away you start in...

> *Aimée returns through the porch. Modeste is hanging up the clothes in the courtyard.*

AIMEE: That's a very good worker, that fellow. If you'd seen how he emptied the machine...but he sure does have a pong on him!

MARIE-JO: And he's nothing compared to...

CRISTELLE: I can't believe you! I must be dreaming...that's awful!

MARIE-JO: That'll be enough out of you. You missed the latest... Miss says she's going to kill herself.

AIMEE: What's the matter, honey-bun?

MARIE-JO: Stop calling her that, she's not a baby.

AIMEE: What am I going to wear?

MARIE-JO: You're fine the way you are.

AIMEE: Well all the same, I'd better take a little light sweater, even if I do sweat.

MARIE-JO: Cristelle, I'm warning you, you'd better straighten up if you want to go to the fair tomorrow evening.

> *Aimée and Marie-Jo exit by the door stage-right. Modeste continues hanging up the laundry in the courtyard. Cristelle rises, goes to the refrigerator, opens it and takes out the bottle of Coca-Cola; she drinks from the bottle.*

CRISTELLE: Modeste, are you thirsty? (*He shakes his head no. Cristelle puts back the bottle.*) Everything okay?

MODESTE: Okay.

> *She goes to the window and looks out for a moment.*

CRISTELLE: Modeste, come here. Quick.

> *Modeste joins her at the window and looks out.*

CRISTELLE: It's for the fair tomorrow. You'll see, there'll be a roller coaster and bumper cars. And then we'll go dancing.

MODESTE: Dancing?

CRISTELLE: We're going to dance.

MODESTE: I can't dance white peoples' dances.

CRISTELLE: Neither can they. It's easy, I'll teach you to dance slow, everyone will look at us. Believe me, these hicks have never seen a black in their lives.

MODESTE: Will there be beautiful women?

CRISTELLE: Yes, but they'll be nothing compared to Awa. There'll be some real doozies, you won't believe your eyes... You pig, it hasn't taken you long to forget your wife.

MODESTE: She's back in N'Dana, and I'm in France.

CRISTELLE: You're all the same. What about Joachim, has he forgotten me?

MODESTE: No, he was jealous because I was coming to see you. When he gave me the T-shirt he had tears in his eyes.

CRISTELLE: I'll never go back to Africa.

MODESTE: Why?

CRISTELLE: My mother said so.

MODESTE: Your country is beautiful, the people are nice.

CRISTELLE: They're dumb.

MODESTE: There's no dust, no sand.

CRISTELLE: And there's no desert wind, either...it's awful, no Harmattan. So you like it here?

MODESTE: Yes, I'm very happy.

CRISTELLE: Good. You can take presents back for your kids, and a beautiful dress for Awa. See that old woman, her name's Marie Jules, she's the town crazy.

MODESTE: Is it true that the whites don't take care of their old people?

CRISTELLE: Yes, they throw them away.

Raymond enters, stage right, carrying a rifle and a revolver in his right hand.

RAYMOND: Where have the girls got to?

CRISTELLE: They're upstairs.

RAYMOND: Here, Sambo, take a look.

CRISTELLE: That's not funny, Grandpa. It's stupid.

RAYMOND: Ever seen anything like that, fella?

CRISTELLE: He goes hunting with Dad in the bush.

RAYMOND: So he knows how to shoot?

MODESTE: No, Sir.

RAYMOND: Come on, I'll teach you.

Raymond goes into the courtyard. Modeste follows. Cristelle returns to the recliner on the porch. Raymond leans the rifle against a wall and shows Modeste how to hold the revolver and fires at a target, which is out of sight. He hands Modeste the gun.

RAYMOND: Here, give me your hand. Put your finger here, like that. Now, extend your arm. Now aim at the board and fire. Go on, fire. Bring your arm lower. Come on, lean into it — you're not much on the ball, are you?

CRISTELLE: I'd like to see you hunting wild boar in the forest with nothing but a pointed stick, we'd see how on the ball you are.

37

RAYMOND: Don't be afraid, fire. (*Modeste fires.*) Too high. Watch how I do it.

> *Raymond fires. Aimée dashes in. She has a cardigan over her shoulders.*

AIMEE: Stop all that horsing around. He thinks he's John Wayne! Raymond, that's enough...the neighbors...

RAYMOND: It's my house, isn't it? Go on, pal, shoot it.

> *He hands the revolver to Modeste. Marie-Jo enters, wearing a white skirt, white shirt, white sandals and a small black-leather shoulder bag.*

MARIE-JO: Papa, take that thing back. Bob doesn't like him handling guns.

AIMEE: Poor guy, he's scared stiff. And you're keeping him from his work.

MARIE-JO: And as for you, you big slug, get upstairs and change that T-shirt right this minute.

AIMEE: It *isn't* very attractive, is it? Look at his teeth, I'd be scared.

CRISTELLE: You think your face isn't scary?

MARIE-JO: Will you do as I say, for Chrissake? Off you go!

> *Cristelle rises and exits, stage right. Modeste returns to hanging the clothes on the line. Raymond comes onto the porch, carrying the rifle in one hand, the revolver in the other.*

AIMEE: Are you off your nut?

MARIE-JO: Bob doesn't like that.

AIMEE: I can see why.

RAYMOND: He's hopeless.

AIMEE: All the more reason.

MARIE-JO: What are we having for supper?

AIMEE: We were thinking of a shoulder roast with potato casserole.

MARIE-JO: Modeste, peel the potatoes for tonight's supper.

MODESTE: Yes, Ma'am.

AIMEE: They're in the little pantry there, beneath the stairs.

MARIE-JO: Are we off?

RAYMOND: And why do you have to tag along, may I ask?

AIMEE: You must be kidding, I never go anywhere. And you never know, old-lady Bothorel may want some curtains run up. Go back to your TV.

RAYMOND: It's some woman's program.

AIMEE: What about your serial?

RAYMOND: That's over.

AIMEE: What time is it? Heavens, already! See you later.

> *Aimée and Marie-Jo exit, stage left. Raymond puts the revolver and the carbine on the table, goes to the refrigerator, opens it, removes some chocolate and takes a bite. He crosses the room, passing the window, and exits stage right, leaving the door open. He returns after a moment carrying a pile of magazines like "Playboy" and "Hustler." He sets them on the table, returns to take the whole bar of chocolate from the refrigerator, and then sits down opposite his usual place. He begins leafing through the magazines while eating his chocolate. Modeste has finished hanging the*

wash and reenters the room, removing his blue apron and hanging it next to the refrigerator.

RAYMOND: Here, fella, take a look at this. (*Modeste comes over to him.*) Ever seen anything like that? Aren't white women beautiful? Get a load of that — and what about that...have you ever seen knockers like that? And what about this one? Have they got women as beautiful as that back where you come from?

MODESTE: I don't know.

RAYMOND: What do you mean, you don't know? And get a look at those two dykes, real S&M types. You know what dykes are?

MODESTE: No, sir.

RAYMOND: That's dykes. A couple of tootsies messing around with each other. And that's nothing...when I was on the Police Rescue Squad, we used to really see things: bottles up the ass, faggots stuck together, sometimes we could hardly keep a straight face, I can tell you! And get a load of this one — that's real one hundred per cent made in Africa, that one. That's what I call a real nice ass, round and firm. I'll bet your wife's got a real nice ass, she must have, to have seven kids?

MODESTE: Where are the potatoes, Sir?

RAYMOND: There, under the stairs.

> *He points to the closet. Modeste goes to it and bends to open the latch; he begins rummaging around inside. Cristelle enters by the door, stage right, hitting Modeste in the process. Raymond quickly slips his magazines out of sight.*

CRISTELLE: I'm sorry, I didn't know you were there. Did I hurt you?

MODESTE: No.

CRISTELLE: Have they gone?

RAYMOND: Good riddance.

> *Cristelle goes to the window; she is wearing a pair of small, tight-fitting shorts and a tank top. Raymond rises to exit, stage right, carrying his magazines.*

RAYMOND: You've changed clothes again?

CRISTELLE: Yes, I was too hot.

RAYMOND: Well, no danger of that now.

> *Raymond exits. Modeste has found the basket of potatoes, which he places on the table.*

CRISTELLE: Come on, Modeste, let me teach you how to dance.

MODESTE: No.

CRISTELLE: Why not? It's easy, you'll see. It's like they do it at Aunt Angèle's place, you've seen them haven't you?

MODESTE: Yes.

> *Cristelle comes up to him.*

CRISTELLE: So there's nothing to it. You put your arm there, like that, and take my hand with the other one, and then you just move a little.

> *She begins to hum "La vie en rose" and to dance.*

MODESTE: You could clean the whole kitchen with the amount of soap you used.

CRISTELLE: (*imitating her grandmother*) You just need a drop. (*She continues to dance.*) You see, it's not all that hard... You'll drive them crazy tomorrow.

> *She goes on humming. They laugh as they dance, while the curtain slowly falls. Line Renaud can be heard singing "La vie en rose" in Japanese.*

DAY THREE

Evening. It is dark outside and still hot; the porch door is open. Aimée, Raymond and Marie-Jo are seated around the table. Marie-Jo sits at one end, her back to the porch; she is wearing a sleeveless white cotton dress with a slightly revealing neckline. She is engaged in writing a long letter. Aimée and Raymond are playing dominos, seated at their usual places. They are dressed as before.

AIMEE: It's your turn.

RAYMOND: No it's not, it's yours.

AIMEE: Excuse me, but I put down the double three. Draw.

RAYMOND: I pass.

AIMEE: Double blank, draw... Raymond, are you asleep or what?

RAYMOND: I pass.

AIMEE: I can't believe it, I've won again! That means that you must be seeing someone else behind my back!

RAYMOND: I wish!

AIMEE: I'll bet! Well, don't let me stop you.

MARIE-JO: I'd like to see the look on your face if he really did!

AIMEE: You're both nuts. That kind of thing doesn't interest me any more. In fact, I'll tell you something: The whole idea disgusts me.

RAYMOND: You didn't used to talk like that.

AIMEE: No, I didn't, but I do now. And stop looking at me that way, you'll get over it... Shall we play another round?

RAYMOND: Sure.

MARIE-JO: Do you play dominos every day?

AIMEE: Don't ask! You should see us in the wintertime, we're like two bumps on a log — the shutters are closed at five, dominos or cards until six forty-five, supper, and at seven-twenty the local TV program for your dad.

RAYMOND: What else are we supposed to do?

AIMEE: Exactly.

MARIE-JO: What would you say if you were in my shoes?

AIMEE: It's your decision, not mine.

MARIE-JO: We may leave Africa next year.

RAYMOND: To go where?

MARIE-JO: Brazil.

RAYMOND: De Gaulle said the Brazilians were stupid.

MARIE-JO: He must not have seen the blacks.

AIMEE: This morning down at the bakery old lady Lachiver says to me: "Your son-in-law didn't come this year? I saw Marie-Jo at the mall with..." I cut her right off: "Oh yes, of course, with her boy." She just stood there with a dumb expression on her face. What a loud mouth she is...always into other people's business. At least in Paris...

RAYMOND: Listen, are you playing? Shit or get off the pot!

AIMEE: I beg your pardon! What kind of language is that?

RAYMOND: You keep harping on it...

AIMEE: Well, that takes the cake...will you listen to him? "Harping," is it?

Marie-Jo gets up, goes to the refrigerator, takes out a beer and gets a glass from the buffet.

MARIE-JO: Do you want something to drink, Dad?

AIMEE: Well! And I suppose I'm invisible!

MARIE-JO: You don't even give me time to ask...

AIMEE: Nothing for me, thanks. The more you drink, the thirstier you get.

MARIE-JO: Dad?

AIMEE: What a question!

MARIE-JO: Will you lay off? Dad?

RAYMOND: I'll have what you're having.

She takes another glass from the buffet and another beer from the refrigerator.

AIMEE: While you're up, I'll have some chocolate.

MARIE-JO: There isn't any.

AIMEE: That you bought yesterday?

MARIE-JO: It's gone...Cristelle must have eaten it.

AIMEE: I don't think so, she only likes the dark.

RAYMOND: It must have been him.

MARIE-JO: I'd be surprised, he never does a thing without asking permission... It drives Bob wild.

RAYMOND: Yeah, he's a little candy-assed, isn't he?

AIMEE: You should talk! *I* think he's very nice. If you'd seen him at the mall, his eyes nearly popped out of his head! And when you bought him that pair of white pants and that shirt, you should have seen the expression on his face! It reminded me of Pirate.

MARIE-JO: He's great.

> *She sets a beer and a glass in front of Raymond and goes back to sit down at her place.*

AIMEE: And he's so good at everything, he irons better than a woman...the man's a real jewel.

MARIE-JO: I taught him everything he knows. If you saw where he comes from...

RAYMOND: He's a real jungle bunny, that's obvious.

AIMEE: That's obvious, that's obvious... And what about the people around here, where do you think they come from? Straight from the backwoods, that's where — they all still have straw sticking out of their ears and shit on their shoes.

MARIE-JO: But when you see what's happened to Paris, you wouldn't want to live there, either.

RAYMOND: You can say that again, there's nothing but wogs, niggers and chinks. After dark there's not a real French person on the street.

AIMEE: Of course, it's no better here. The cafe next door is Portuguese, and out where they're building the new highway it's all Arabs and Turks.

RAYMOND: They're only temporary.

AIMEE: That didn't keep the city from asking people to take them in last winter because it was so cold in those trailers they live in.

RAYMOND: They didn't ask us.

AIMEE: They're not crazy...they know what we think.

MARIE-JO: What's this new mayor like?

AIMEE: He's a dope, *and* a communist, used to be a school principal. He really thinks he's something, that one.

RAYMOND: He raised the local taxes. Him and his whole bunch got in...now they do whatever they want.

AIMEE: You'll see how they carry on on the fourteenth of July. It's really too bad — the rest of France is voting right, and here we're stuck with the commies.

RAYMOND: It's always like that.

AIMEE: That's what I said. What's it like in Brazil?

MARIE-JO: I don't know.

RAYMOND: In South America, they've got the army.

AIMEE: And a good thing, too. And what about Cristelle, will you be taking her with you?

MARIE-JO: Certainly not. She'll stay in France...she needs some- one to keep an eye on her, boarding school is good for her. You heard what her principal told me today...

AIMEE: Poor honey.

MARIE-JO: She asked for it, she's a lazy slug and all she thinks

47

about is having fun. I want her to go on to college.

RAYMOND: You're right.

MARIE-JO: She'll thank me for it later on. If I hadn't met Bob, I'd still be working in that factory.

AIMEE: Yes, but you always did just what you pleased.

MARIE-JO: You're the one who wanted me to find a job after I got my diploma.

AIMEE: Raymond, do you hear that? That takes the cake! *I* wanted you to be a nurse.

MARIE-JO: So I could marry a doctor.

AIMEE: I never said that.

MARIE-JO: You've got a short memory. *I* wanted to be a beautician.

AIMEE: That wasn't considered real job in those days.

MARIE-JO: "All beauticians are hookers, you'd better get a real job." I've never forgotten that.

AIMEE: That was your father.

RAYMOND: Me?

MARIE-JO: No, it was you, and I've never gotten over it. It was the same when I got married.

AIMEE: I like Bob.

RAYMOND: Yeah, now you do.

AIMEE: Okay, spineless, that's enough.

MARIE-JO: He's right. You like him all right...now.

AIMEE: Oh, he's always right. Good night.

She exits through the door, stage right. Raymond slowly begins to return the dominoes to their box.

MARIE-JO: What a temper!

RAYMOND: Who are you telling?

MARIE-JO: She's not getting any better with age.

RAYMOND: It's been worse since we lost Pirate.

MARIE-JO: A dog — you can always get another one.

RAYMOND: You tell her that if you really want to see her get mad.

MARIE-JO: It must be kind of hard to put up with every day.

RAYMOND: You can say that again...she's always got some bug up her ass.

MARIE-JO: Don't let her get you down.

Raymond rises and puts the box of dominoes on the shelf behind him. He takes his glass and bottle and goes to the sink. He throws the bottle into the trash and rinses out the glass, setting it on the drain board.

RAYMOND: We could have had such a peaceful retirement...

MARIE-JO: That's true.

RAYMOND: Well, time to turn in.

He goes to Marie-Jo, bends over and kisses her.

49

MARIE-JO: Goodnight, Dad.

RAYMOND: Goodnight. Say hello to Bob for us.

MARIE-JO: Sure.

He exits, stage right. Marie-Jo returns to her letter. After a moment she rises, takes her empty bottle and puts it in the trash. She goes to the refrigerator, takes another beer and returns to her seat. She rereads her letter and finishes it. She rises, puts the letter on the buffet, puts the paper and envelopes away in one of the drawers, returns to the table, refills her glass with beer and throws the empty bottle in the trash. She turns out the center lamp and turns on the porch light. She takes her glass and goes out to sit in the recliner on the porch. She gets up again, takes a magazine from the buffet and returns to the porch. She begins to leaf through "Elle." After a pause the door, stage left, opens softly. Modeste enters. He is wearing white trousers, a white Lacoste-type shirt and white tennis shoes. He is carrying a large Kewpie doll, a white glass vase and a bottle of sparkling wine.

MARIE-JO: Is that you?

MODESTE: It's me, Ma'am.

MARIE-JO: Where's Cristelle?

MODESTE: She'll be along.

MARIE-JO: What do you mean, "she'll be along?"

MODESTE: She said "I'll be along."

MARIE-JO: That kid! Was she with that wog?

MODESTE: I don't know.

MARIE-JO: You could see who she was with, couldn't you?

MODESTE: There was a lot of folks.

MARIE-JO: What's all that?

MODESTE: I won the drawing.

MARIE-JO: Aren't you the lucky one!

MODESTE: Would you like the champagne?

MARIE-JO: No, you keep it for yourself.

MODESTE: I don't drink. I'll give it to the old folks tomorrow, as a present.

MARIE-JO: Yes, they'll like that a lot.

He sets the bottle on the table.

MODESTE: The doll, that's for my house.

MARIE-JO: It's pretty. And what about the vase?

MODESTE: That's for Mamadou, God willing.

MARIE-JO: You'd better put them away.

MODESTE: Tomorrow I'm going to win the radio.

He exits, stage right, carrying the doll and the vase. Marie-Jo goes back to her magazine, sipping her beer. The door has remained open.

MARIE-JO: Modeste...

Modeste returns after a brief pause.

MARIE-JO: So, tell me what the fair was like.

MODESTE: I went on one of the rides with Cristelle.

MARIE-JO: The roller coaster, the one that goes round?

MODESTE: Yes, it's very fast.

MARIE-JO: Were you scared?

MODESTE: No.

MARIE-JO: Not even a little bit?

MODESTE: Yes, in the cars that touch...

MARIE-JO: The bumper cars. Did you go to the dance?

MODESTE: Yes.

MARIE-JO: Did you dance?

MODESTE: Once, with Cristelle.

MARIE-JO: Did you make out with anyone? (*Modeste grins.*) Well, you've still got time, the fair is on for three days. You can go to bed, I'll wait up for her. Good night. Pleasant dreams.

MODESTE: Good night.

> *He exits, stage right, without shutting the door. Thirty seconds later he returns and stands motionless in the doorway. Marie-Jo, still lying in the recliner, does not see him, since her back is turned to him. She finishes her beer and rises. She gives a start when she sees Modeste standing in the shadows.*

MARIE-JO: You scared me! What's the matter?

MODESTE: Ma'am, I need you.

MARIE-JO: What?

MODESTE: I need you.

MARIE-JO: What for?

MODESTE: I need you.

MARIE-JO: I heard you, but why? What do you mean?

MODESTE: I'm horny.

MARIE-JO: Careful now — what kind of talk is that? What's got into you, you must be crazy. Have you been drinking? Take a good look at me, Modeste — I'm white. Turn on the light.

He presses the light switch next to the door, the main light comes on. Marie-Jo sets her glass on the table.

MARIE-JO: Well, I'll be... So the man's horny. That takes the cake... What's got into you?

Marie-Jo approaches the doorway where Modeste is standing.

MARIE-JO: Move aside. Dad! Dad! I can't believe this! Take a good look at me, Modeste. I'm a racist — get it? I don't like blacks and I never will. You're all uncivilized, you're all backward...you all disgust me, and that includes you too. You could knock me over with a feather — I never expected *this!* Ugh!

Raymond enters. He is wearing the same beige cloth pants and now has on a striped pajama top.

RAYMOND: What's going on?

MARIE-JO: It seems this gentleman wants to sleep with me.

RAYMOND: What!

MARIE-JO: I make him horny, and I quote.

RAYMOND: Come over here, fella. Come on! Just say that so I can hear you! Come on...swallowed your tongue or something?

You know, I've gone up against bigger guys than you. Come on, out with it!

MODESTE: Excuse...

RAYMOND: Excuse...fuck your excuses, that's not what I'm asking you.

MARIE-JO: You won't get anything out of him, they're all stubborn as mules.

RAYMOND: We'll see about that. I wasn't in Indochina for nothing. Sit down.

> *Raymond takes a chair and pushes Modeste into it. Aimée enters wearing a short flimsy nightgown that leaves her arms bare. Marie-Jo and Raymond ignore her, but Modeste stares at her.*

AIMEE: Modeste, honey, what's going on, you look pale... Is he sick?

RAYMOND: Okay, out with it. Let's hear you say it.

AIMEE: Did someone attack him?

RAYMOND: You must be kidding...he's the one doing the attacking.

AIMEE: Who?

MARIE-JO: Me.

RAYMOND: He tried to get her into bed.

AIMEE: What are you talking about?

MARIE-JO: It's true.

AIMEE: Has he been drinking?

MARIE-JO: No...but he tried to make me drink some champagne.

AIMEE: What champagne?

MARIE-JO: That champagne. He won it at the fair.

AIMEE: You call that champagne — it's cat piss, a real nigger drink. Have you gone crazy or what?

RAYMOND: We're not in Africa now. We whites, we believe in sticking to one woman, and we don't eat each other, either. I ought to cut it off.

AIMEE: That's right, your wife might have some peace then. Seven children, just like rabbits...if you even know what a rabbit is?

MARIE-JO: And I trusted him.

AIMEE: Well, not me. I said to your father at the beginning, "That one's got something up his sleeve." Didn't I, Raymond?

RAYMOND: Yes. (*To Marie-Jo*) What are you going to do?

AIMEE: We're going to call the police.

MARIE-JO: Oh, no we're not! We'll just send him back where he came from.

AIMEE: Right away?

MARIE-JO: First thing tomorrow morning, taxi, train to Paris, straight onto the plane. He's got an open ticket.

AIMEE: And until tomorrow? I won't be able to get a wink of sleep.

RAYMOND: I'll take care of him.

He goes to the refrigerator and takes out a beer.

AIMEE: What a mess! After all you've done for him.

MARIE-JO: And Bob — I'd like to see his face when he hears about this.

MODESTE: I'll ask Mr. Bob to give me his pardon.

MARIE-JO: You do that if you want to have him rearrange your face.

AIMEE: He needs more than a good going over—he should go to prison.

Raymond goes over to Modeste and gives him a shove.

RAYMOND: Stand up.

MARIE-JO: Look out, Dad.

RAYMOND: Don't worry. (*He moves over to the closet beneath the stairs.*) I said, stand up!

MARIE-JO: Do what he says, Modeste.

RAYMOND: Come here. (*Modeste rises and goes over to him.*) Down on your knees! (*Modeste kneels on the floor.*) Open the door. Take all the stuff out.

> *On his hands and knees Modeste begins to empty the closet: the basket of potatoes, newspapers, old kitchen utensils, including a pan for grilling chestnuts. Aimée takes it from him.*

AIMEE: So that's where it's been! I looked for it everywhere, last winter...

> *The door, stage left, opens quietly. Cristelle enters; she is wearing a short T-shirt dress.*

CRISTELLE: You still hunting for that rat?

MARIE-JO: Do you know what time it is? Why didn't you come home with him?

CRISTELLE: I ran into Katell and Nathalie.

MARIE-JO: I told you to come back together.

CRISTELLE: It's only been five minutes...

MARIE-JO: Exactly.

RAYMOND: Come on, Rastus, let's go!

CRISTELLE: What's got into you?

AIMEE: This son-of-bitch tried to rape your mother.

CRISTELLE: She didn't let him?

MARIE-JO: Stupid!

RAYMOND: Come on, in you go!

MODESTE: No, Sir.

RAYMOND: (*giving him a shove*) I said, get in there!

MODESTE: No.

CRISTELLE: Leave him alone.

> *Raymond exits, stage right.*

AIMEE: He's dangerous.

CRISTELLE: Dangerous! What about you all? Don't let them do it, Modeste.

MARIE-JO: You mind your own business.

CRISTELLE: It's a pity he didn't!

MARIE-JO: You little shit!

Marie-Jo slaps her. Modeste takes advantage of their altercation to go onto the porch.

CRISTELLE: You've no right to do that.

MARIE-JO: You don't even know what happened.

CRISTELLE: So, tell me.

AIMEE: He tried to rape her.

CRISTELLE: Were you there? I know Modeste.

MARIE-JO: That's enough! No kid is going to tell us what to do. Get up to bed.

CRISTELLE: You're disgusting, all of you!

MARIE-JO: Upstairs, I said!

Marie-Jo shoves Cristelle towards the door, stage right.

CRISTELLE: Ugly bitch!

Raymond reenters carrying his rifle.

CRISTELLE: Are you crazy?

MARIE-JO: Out! (*She pushes Cristelle out and exits with her.*)

RAYMOND: Where is he?

AIMEE: Out on the porch. Watch out...

Raymond goes to the sliding door. Modeste is standing in the doorway looking out.

RAYMOND: Turn around.

Modeste turns around and Raymond points the rifle at him.

RAYMOND: Hands on your head! I said, hands on your head! You won't be the first... Now, move! (*Modeste moves forward, hands on his head.*) Over to the closet! (*Modeste goes to the closet, Raymond behind him.*) In you go! I said: Get in!

Modeste gets down on his knees and crawls into the closet. Raymond closes the door and turns the latch.

AIMEE: What a night! My knees are shaking.

She sits down at the stage-left side of the table. Marie-Jo reenters.

MARIE-JO: Where is he?

RAYMOND: In the hole.

AIMEE: What about the kid?

MARIE-JO: She's gone crazy. I locked her in her room. I'm thirsty.

She goes to the refrigerator, takes out a beer and swigs it down. Raymond gets a chair and sets it in front of the closet door, leaning his rifle against the wall.

RAYMOND: Me too.

He goes to the refrigerator and takes out a beer.

MARIE-JO: I'm going back upstairs. You never know what she'll get up to.

AIMEE: Raymond, will you take that charm off? I can say it now —it makes you look ridiculous.

RAYMOND: What about that bracelet?

AIMEE: Sorry, but it's not the same thing...mine's ivory.

MARIE-JO: Sure it is — ivory plastic.

AIMEE: Really? I always thought so myself...

MARIE-JO: I'm going upstairs. We'll be able to think better tomorrow. Goodnight.

RAYMOND: Goodnight, sweetheart.

AIMEE: Don't be too hard on her. Goodnight.

>*Marie-Jo exits, stage right.*

AIMEE: What a night! I don't think I'll be able to sleep...

RAYMOND: Take a pill.

AIMEE: You're right.

>*She takes a pill from the buffet and washes it down with some of her husband's beer.*

RAYMOND: You go on up. I'm afraid they're going to get into it, those two.

AIMEE: I'm off. What about you?

RAYMOND: I'd better stay here, just in case.

AIMEE: Sit in the recliner, you'll be more comfy.

RAYMOND: Don't worry. Go on.

AIMEE: What a nightmare! Let's hope things will get back to normal tomorrow. Goodnight.

RAYMOND: 'Night.

> *Aimée exits stage right. Raymond turns out the main light, leaving only the porch light lit. He sits down on the chair in front of the closet door and lays his rifle across his knees. The curtain falls slowly.*

∾

NOTES ON THE CHARACTERS

The GRANDFATHER. 62 years old. Name: Raymond.
The third in a family of seven (five boys, two girls). Son of Pierre-Marie Moisant, a cabinet-maker in a village in Brittany, and Eugénie Droniou, housewife.
At fourteen he passes his school-leaving certificate.
At eighteen, with one of his uncles, a deep-sea fisherman, he joins General de Gaulle in England. His devotion to the General will be lifelong. After the war, he joins the police force in Paris and becomes a city policeman. In the summer of 1946 he returns to Brittany in hopes of marrying his cousin, Guiguitte, but finds that she had already accepted the proposal of a young doctor.
He returns to Paris and begins seeing Aimée, a girl with a Breton background who works in the cafeteria at police headquarters. Six months later they get married and move into a small apartment south of Montparnasse. A few months later their first child, Louis, is born; a sickly infant, he dies at the age of two. A year later, Marie-Jo is born, a sturdy girl who will be her father's pride and joy. Every year the family spends a month in Brittany, where they rent a small house.
During the Algerian War, Raymond takes a leave of absence from the police force to work as bodyguard for bankers or politicians threatened by the OAS (Organisation d'Armée Sécrète, the underground movement combatting Algerian independence). Around 1968 he moves out to the suburbs south of Paris. At the same time he leaves the active police force and transfers to a desk job at police headquarters. His daughter marries and moves away, first to Brittany and then to Africa. At fifty, Raymond takes early retirement and comes back to live in his hometown in Brittany with his wife, where we find him.

The GRANDMOTHER. 55 years old. Name: Aimée.
Born in the southern part of Paris (14th arrondissement). Father, Antoine Cadiou, employed in the Paris Métro; mother, Armande Geffroy, a dressmaker. Aimée has one brother who is two years older than she.

At fourteen she flunks her school-leaving certificate. She quits school and works as a salesgirl for her mother's sister, who runs a small grocery store in Rue Asseline. At seventeen, thanks to her Uncle Joseph, she finds a job as a waitress in the police headquarters cafeteria. At this juncture she has a secret affair with an Italian named Luigi. She is in love with him, but he is already married; she then accepts the attentions of Raymond, a young policeman. She marries him when she becomes pregnant by the Italian. She quits her job to take care of her child and their little two-room apartment. Through her mother she does some sewing for people in the neighborhood. The death of her son, a sickly child, comes as almost a relief but nevertheless makes her very unhappy (she cannot help thinking of him as the child of her sin).

The birth of her daughter sets things right again.

Like her husband, she worships General de Gaulle. She is not thrilled by her daughter's marriage to a boy from Brittany with a checkered background, but she soon changes her mind and now adores her son-in-law.

She is not yet forty-five years old when her husband decides to retire, to "bury himself" in Brittany. She loathes it there, but there is nothing she can do. His pension is not very large and they have trouble making ends meet. Aside from her husband's cousin Guiguitte, she has no friends in the town. She considers the natives backward and "retarded," and is convinced that Paris has everything, Brittany nothing. She continues to do sewing jobs, for which she is paid under the table.

The MOTHER. 35 years of age. Name: Marie-Jo.
An outwardly ordinary childhood with a father who spoils her —"rotten," as the saying goes — and a mother whom she early begins to think of as "Mrs. Don't-Do-That." As a child she is the neighborhood dictator and a bit of a bully. The fact that she is a policeman's daughter doesn't bother her at all; to the contrary, she holds it over her friends: "My dad's a cop." At each school holiday she goes to Brittany to stay with her paternal grandparents. She'd like to stay there all year, since she thinks it is heaven on earth. She remains in school through junior high school, just managing to pass the exams for her diploma. Her parents, espe-

cially her mother, want her to continue with her schooling and "make something of herself," but Marie-Jo would prefer to go to work in Brittany to be with her boyfriend, Gilbert, a science student.

In the end, however, she stays in Paris and works as a salesgirl in a department store. She spends every weekend with Gilbert in Rennes, where he is studying. One year, during Christmas vacation, Marie-Jo meets Bob, Gilbert's elder brother, who has come home after a ten-year absence (he had joined the Army at 18). They fall in love at first sight and get married two months later. At first, Bob has trouble settling down and finds such jobs as pumping gas at a service station, driving a truck, etc. After the birth of their daughter, Cristelle, they both find jobs as assembly-line workers in a factory that makes communications products. Three years later they are both promoted to the post of foreman. Responding to an ad in a newspaper, they leave Brittany for Africa (Ivory Coast), where Bob finds a very good job as personnel director in a sugar refinery. Marie-Jo stops working. The company provides them with a large house and swimming pool. She has servants and her new life suits her. She likes Africa, but not the Africans.

The DAUGHTER. 16 years of age. Name: Cristelle.
A love child, not a mistake. She has always been a disappointment to her parents. They had hoped for a boy and find themselves saddled with a "bratty girl" who arrives two months prematurely after a painful delivery that nearly kills her mother and, according to her, prevents her from having any more children. Her early years are difficult ones and she is often sick (bronchitis, earaches, diarrhea). She is almost four years old when she is taken to Ivory Coast. Since her parents live outside of town, her mother teaches her to read and write when she has the time. Cristelle is often alone; the other children in the white community live at some distance from the refinery, and she rarely sees them.

At ten she is sent to school in Katiola, where her mother drives her each day. She is the only white child in the class. She has trouble studying but otherwise has a very good time in school. Finally she has some friends. Every year she spends the two summer months in Brittany with her grandparents, her father and her mother. She is bored there, but she is happy to be able to return to Africa with new clothes and presents for her friends.

At 15 she falls in love with Joachim Outtara, 21 years of age, the son of the sub-prefect at Katiola. After a few months, the parents learn of their affair and all hell breaks loose. She is sent back to Brittany to stay with her grandparents and put into a boarding school run by nuns.

The SERVANT. 36 years of age. Name: Modeste.

The ninth in a family of eleven children.

Has always lived in his native village, N'Dana, not far from the sugar refinery. The son of small farmers (a small cotton field, a few chickens and a plot of land for growing vegetables), he attends the school at the edge of the village, which has only two classes. He remains there until the age of 12. Thanks to the bus run by the sugar refinery he is able to continue his schooling in Katiola. At 16 he is forced to find a job and begins working at the refinery. He is a hard worker, punctual and disciplined. After two years he is hired as a servant at the villa of the new white manager's family.

At 22 he marries Awa, 16 years old, also from N'Dana. He continues to work as a servant. In the evenings he returns to his hut around 10 p.m. and at 6 a.m. he goes back to his employers. He has one day off per week. Awa and he have seven children (five boys, two girls). He has now been working for Marie-Jo and her husband for twelve years. He is the only "boy" his mistress trusts: "He's clean and he doesn't steal." He always accompanies her to Katiola or to Bouaké on market days. His mistress frequently raises her voice to the other blacks, but never to him. She automatically passes their used clothes on to him for himself and his family. After his employers buy a house in France they decide to take him along with them when they return there for the summer. He will be able to help them to clear the property and get things ready for them to move in. He leaves ahead of time with his mistress; the master of the house is to join them two weeks later.

For him, this represents a great adventure.